Also available in this series from Quadrille:

the little book of

REST

Quadrille

Rest

Definition:

verb

1. To (cause someone or something to) stop doing a particular activity or stop being active for a period of time in order to relax and recover your strength.

2. A word of uncertain origin, rest [sleep, repose, slumber] derives from the Old English *ræste*, *reste* and Proto-Germanic *rasto* – also of Old Saxon resta: resting place.

Rest, otherwise known as...

Chilling

Downtime

Hanging loose

R&R

Taking five

Taking it easy

Unwinding

" *Take rest; a field that has rested gives a bountiful crop.*"

OVID

Restful questions to ask ourselves

When did I rest last month?

When did I rest last week?

When did I rest yesterday?

How shall I rest today?

How shall I rest next week?

How shall I rest next month?

How to use the morning sun to usher in a wakeful morning

1. Open blinds and curtains before going to bed.

2. Use a sunrise alarm clock or light therapy lamp to gently increase light exposure.

3. Set an intention to wake up within an hour of sunrise.

4. Within the first hour of waking, spend five to 10 minutes outside in the morning light (10–20 minutes might be needed on cloudy days).

Five morning mantras to encourage a restful mindset

- I am grateful for the gift of sleep and wake rested and recharged.

- I am grateful for whatever energy levels I have and will recharge when I need to.

- Today I will approach each task with gentle and efficient energy.

- I give myself permission to stop and reset when my body or mind needs a break.

- This morning, I embrace a balance of work, rest and pleasure.

" *The town was glad with morning light; places that had shown ugly and distrustful all night long, now wore a smile; and sparkling sunbeams dancing on chamber windows, and twinkling through blind and curtain before sleepers' eyes, shed light even into dreams, and chased away the shadows of the night.* "

CHARLES DICKENS
The Old Curiosity Shop

When his friend James Boswell visited lexicographer Samuel Johnson in the morning, Johnson shouted down to his chum, "Let us breakfast in splendour." A fine feast followed that took hours to work through.

Elevate commonplace activities such as breakfast into an occasion in order to set a more restful pace for the day. Why rush? Why hurry? Why not kick back, summon a friend, order coffee and decide to 'breakfast in splendour'?

" You can't imagine what a pleasure this complete laziness is to me: not a thought in my brain – you might send a ball rolling through it! "

LEO TOLSTOY
Anna Karenina

" *The animals well knew that Badger, having eaten a hearty breakfast, had retired to his study and settled himself in an arm-chair with his legs up on another and a red cotton handkerchief over his face, and was being 'busy' in the usual way at this time of the year.*"

KENNETH GRAHAME
The Wind in the Willows

Rest welcomes phone-free...

Dining

Comfort breaks

Walks

Conversations

Bedrooms

Three easy micro-breaks

1. **Pause for at least 30 seconds with your eyes closed before eating.** Use this time to say a simple grace or note of gratitude, or simply embrace the peace this moment brings before enjoying a convivial meal.

2. **Insist that coffee breaks only involve coffee.** Don't use the break to check the news or your feed, simply savour every mouthful of the drink in peace and quiet.

3. **Wait for at least 30 seconds before leaving the house.** Close your eyes and centre your scattered senses for a moment before embarking on the day.

" Nothing could be more pleasant than to live in solitude, enjoy the spectacle of nature, and occasionally read some book."

NIKOLAI GOGOL

How to curate the perfect lie-in

1. Ensure there are no commitments until midday at the earliest.

2. Arrange necessary child and pet care.

3. Remove all digital devices from the bedroom.

4. Firmly close all doors and curtains.

5. Don't ruin the possibility of a lie-in with an outrageously late, drunken night out.

6. Sleep, sleep, sleep and sleep.

7. Savour that delicious feeling of waking up and slowly appreciating that you are able to go back to sleep if you so desire.

" Nobody can bring you peace but yourself. "

RALPH WALDO EMERSON

" Sometimes the most important thing in a whole day is the rest we take between two deep breaths, or the turning inwards in prayer for five short minutes. **"**

ETTY HILLESUM

Three quick ways to rest for five minutes

1. Leave your phone in another room and sit in darkness with your eyes closed, until your breathing has become peaceful and your mind has stopped chattering.

2. Leave your phone inside and stand outside. Turn your face to the sun, feel its warmth and breathe deeply.

3. Just stop now. Put this book down and wait, in peace, for five minutes.

In 2016 a survey of 18,000 individuals across 135 countries for BBC Radio 4 asked participants their favourite restful activities. Consider the list – do you agree? What is missing? What would you find most restful?

1. Reading

2. Listening to music

3. Spending time in nature

4. Taking a bath or shower

5. Meditation or mindfulness

6. Physical exercise

7. Chatting with friends or family

8. Drinking alcohol

9. Watching TV

10. Eating

How to accelerate rest

Detach yourself from
your phone and just 'be'.

Questions to ask ourselves about rest

Have I got the work–rest
balance right?

Am I resting to work
or working to rest?

Would more rest improve
my productive life?

" *I believe the nicest and sweetest days are not those on which anything very splendid or wonderful or exciting happens but just those that bring simple little pleasures, following one another softly, like pearls slipping off a string.* "

LUCY MAUD MONTGOMERY
Anne of Green Gables

In the song 'Tomorrow Never Knows', Beatles singer John Lennon implored people who felt beset with doubt to turn off their minds, relax and float downstream.

The 10 most relaxing pieces of music according to Classic FM

Morning Mood, Grieg

Primavera, Einaudi

Air on the G String, Bach

War Song, Phamie Gow

Gymnopédie No.1, Satie

'Children's Intermezzo' from Othello, Coleridge-Taylor

Clair de Lune, Debussy

Spiegel im Spiegel, Pärt

Romeo and Juliet, Craig Armstrong

Wiegenlied (Lullaby), Brahms

Dare to try the unscheduled break

- Throw caution to the wind and just walk out into the sunshine.

- Down tools saying, "I need a breather, I'll be back soon."

- Rest for as long as you can resist the pull to return.

But how do I know if I am resting?

1. You are not worrying or planning.

2. Your mind is not drawn to work or family worries.

3. You are not trying to control the situation.

4. You are enjoying yourself.

But I'm an extrovert –
I don't need to rest!

Always surrounded with people or digital chatter, extroverts sometimes find it unnecessary to sit in peace, alone – not when there's a party to go to! If this chimes with you, reframe rest as training or preparation for even greater social brilliance.

Five ways for extroverts to rest

1. Schedule one-hour rest time; that way it will at least feel business-like.

2. Choose a solitary activity (reading a book, listening to vinyl) that you can share with friends later.

3. Take a pause on initiating social events – see how your diary populates and compare which pace brings you more pleasure.

4. Turn down an invitation (knowing you'll be missed).

5. Leave a party midway through, combining socializing with an early night.

Four ideas for introverts to remember when trying to rest

1. Avoid cabin fever and actively choose a different location to rest.

2. Quiet overthinking by reminding yourself that you, just as much as others, deserve to rest.

3. Understand that relaxing doesn't always need to be enjoyed alone: select like-minded friends for a quiet games night, for instance.

4. Pre-plan a list of relaxation activities and vary them to avoid sinking into an overly solitary routine.

How to relax when feeling fretful

1. Remember there is no need to 'record' this relaxation period on social media – it's OK not to be 'on' all the time.

2. Remind yourself that you are deserving of this relaxation.

3. Choose a relaxing activity that uses your hands to avoid phone checking – baking, sewing or crochet.

4. Calm overactive senses with dimmed lights, candles and drawn curtains.

5. Don't attempt hours of relaxation from a standing start – 20 minutes will do – then stretch out the time gradually as you ease your way into relaxation.

How to relax if you're an alpha

1. Acknowledge you are human and require as much relaxation as the next person.

2. Use your position as 'commander' personality type to model the importance of relaxation to those around you.

3. As with everything, do it properly: when you say you'll be out of contact for an hour, relax for an hour.

4. Give yourself permission to unwind.

5. Park any impatience that you carry and remind yourself that this period of rest will restore energy levels for improved performance afterwards.

When caring for others and organizing rest for yourself, remember...

1. Tell others when you need a rest; don't continue slugging it out until you drop.

2. Be realistic about how much time you will have to yourself.

3. Arrange loving support for those you care for so you can leave them without worry.

4. If possible, try to plan regular breaks into your routine.

5. The break may not come at the time of your choosing, so seize opportunities when they arise.

Five things to do for a loved one to help them relax

1. Make breakfast in bed and... leave them to eat it at leisure.

2. Administer a thorough head, neck and shoulder massage (a real one, not one of those half-hearted affairs delivered in the hope of a return massage).

3. Do their usual chore before they carry it out, even if it's emptying the bins.

4. Run them a warm bubble bath.

5. Offer a foot and lower leg massage while watching a film of their choice.

Rest asks us *not* to...

Keep rushing on

Mistake busyness for being productive

Keep going until we crash

Rest asks us to...

Befriend silence

Be at ease with quiet

Settle into soundless thought

If ever you feel that you're taking too much rest, just tell yourself you're getting in touch with your inner koala. Koalas spend between 20 and 22 hours a day sleeping.

Certain animals take rest seriously by sleeping for many languid hours during the day

Koalas: 20–22 hours

Sloths: 20 hours

Bats: 20 hours

Pythons: 18 hours

Cats: 12–16 hours

Dogs: 12–14 hours

Be more sloth and embrace the desire to ease your way through life

Prioritize sleep, slowly eat leaves, move gently taking care not to disturb your surroundings, and if this all gets a bit much, pause for a rest.

Be inspired by the sleepy sea otters who hold hands when sleeping to create a protective raft

There is a beauty in enjoying communal resting times. Consider creating house rules where there are agreed upon quiet times – for an hour after lunch and then from 8pm, for example. Creating communal sleeping rhythms can strengthen social bonds.

Even busy honey bees need to rest, sleeping between five and eight hours a night. After flexing at the knee, the bees' heads rest towards the floor and their antennae stop moving. Sometimes they are so exhausted that they tip over sideways.

Learn to understand the difference between mental and physical rest and the importance of both.

Questions to ask:

Do I prefer mental or physical rest?

Do I find either easy or challenging?

Why might I be avoiding either?

What can I do to incorporate both into my daily routine?

What does emotional rest mean to you?

- Peace from arguments
- A pause from worry
- The ability not to hide emotions

In a place of comfort, jot down ideas about how a period of emotional rest would play out. Can you picture yourself asking your emotions to stand down for a time? Elaborate on the scene and discover if this act alone calms the emotions.

Three ideas to encourage emotional rest

1. Journalling – write and record before expressing emotions.

2. Seek out those who bring you emotional peace.

3. Discover the pause button. When emotions are high, press pause and get in the habit of saying and doing nothing until heightened emotions have calmed.

Understand cellular rest

Composed of over 30 trillion cells, the human body requires daily sleep to rest and repair. Understanding that, while sleeping, our cells are busy at work repairing themselves can help us to give sleep the priority it deserves.

**While sleeping our
30 trillion cells are busy...**

1. **Protein synthesis:** where new proteins are produced and old proteins repaired.

2. **Mitochondria repair:** the powerhouses of cells require rest and maintenance to ensure optimal energy production.

3. **The production of cytokines –** messenger proteins – that support the immune response and fight infection and inflammation.

Embrace the audacity that comes with saying: "Today I am focusing only on me and my need for rest." The thrill is intoxicating and possibly addictive!

Rest smells like...

The dinner that someone
else is cooking

Hot chocolate and
melting marshmallows

Fresh air and wet dog

The hot wood of a sauna

Rose and geranium bath bubbles

Rest feels like...

Freshly laundered bed linen

The sun on your face with just
the right whisper of breeze

A cat in your lap for
as long as she wants

The joy of no alarm clock

Your lover beside you
with nowhere to go

Rest tastes like...

A hotel breakfast

Coffee savoured, not gulped

A cup of tea in bed

That first sip of Champagne

Dessert... because there's no rush

Rest sounds like...

The clink of ice in a cold drink

Fulfilled silence

Water hissing on the sauna's hot rocks

"Madam, is this pressure OK for your massage?"

Your oldest friend's laughter

Rest sees...

An empty schedule

Good friends at the brunch table

No phone

A wide vista to explore at leisure

A sofa with your name on it

Restful activity

1. Write down your worries before your period of rest.

2. Give yourself permission not to think about them.

3. Embark on your chosen restful activity (sleeping, journalling, forest bathing, jogging).

4. Do not return to your worry.

5. Wait for the solution to present itself to your now rested mind.

" If you can attain repose and calm, believe that you have seized happiness."

JULIE JEANNE ÉLÉONORE
DE LESPINASSE

Learn to unpack how you see rest – do you think that rest is only earned as a *reward* for achieving something? How about considering rest as a *treat* – something unearned but lovely nevertheless. And how about stretching this even further and thinking about rest as something that is *essential,* that needs to happen properly every day?

How to achieve regular digital rest

1. Isolate favourite activities that are possible to do without your phone – such as hiking, going to the gym, watching a film, reading a book.

2. Get in the habit of physically separating from your phone before embarking on the chosen activity.

3. By limiting phone separation to certain activities, rather than attempting a full-scale digital detox, you are more likely to succeed in enjoying phone-free time.

" *Here in my heart, my happiness, my house. Here inside the lighted window is my love, my hope, my life. Peace is my companion on the pathway winding to the threshold. Inside this portal dwells new strength in the security, serenity, and radiance of those I love above life itself. Here two will build new dreams - dreams that tomorrow will come true. The world over, these are the thoughts at eventide when footsteps turn ever homeward. In the haven of the hearthside is rest and peace and comfort.*"

ABRAHAM LINCOLN

Frazzled? On-the-go? Spinning plates? Running on fumes?

If any of these words speak to you, ask yourself how you would like to see your best beloved existing in this state? If it is not acceptable for them, then nor should it be for you.

Q: What is needed for me to switch from a frazzled state to a restful and productive state?

A: To prioritize rest

Find it hard admitting you'd like a few minutes to yourself? Try these lines...

"I'll be right back with you; I just need a few minutes to gather my thoughts."

"Please give me a few moments to refresh myself."

"May we resume this conversation after a 10-minute break?"

We've all heard the quote, "Stress thinks everything is an emergency." Recognizing this is the first step to creating a more restful state. The second step is habitually asking ourselves: is this urgent or non-urgent, when an unexpected event clouds our horizons? True emergencies are thankfully rare.

" There is more to life than increasing its speed."

MAHATMA GANDHI

Ruthlessly timetable rest

Great slabs of work or study are easier to cope with if meaningful rest is already scheduled. Be ruthless about booking in daily breaks, weekly events and fortnight-long holidays. These restful oases in a working desert provide vital inspiration to continue.

Try these creative ways to carve out rest in a work environment

1. Volunteer to care for the office plants. A few minutes watering and spraying greenery is instantly calming.

2. Initiate a two-minute stretching session and invite other colleagues to join from their desks.

3. Be the person who brings in a tray of healthy snacks. That walk around the office sharing them out offers both a physical and mental break as well as a feel-good boost.

"Amid all your duties, keep some hours to yourself."

MARGARET FULLER

Restful tip: avoid scrolling through social media on a work break. Though initially offering of a change of tone and pace from work, social media can provoke emotional exhaustion and diminish rather than revive energy levels.

Don't believe the furious worker bees who insist that rest is sheer laziness. Here's a list of three high achievers who were partial to their beds:

1. Einstein insisted on sleeping 10 hours a night as well as taking naps.

2. Mark Twain famously wrote in bed and is said to have remarked: "I have never taken any exercise, except for eating and resting, and I never intend to take any."

3. Hollywood icon Mae West wrote several of her screenplays in bed, quipping: "Everybody knows I do my best work in bed."

" Go forward while you can, but if your strength fails you, sit down near the road and gaze without anger or envy at those who pass by."

IVAN TURGENEV

Avoid falling into the mindset that says work is more virtuous than rest. Both are important and neither must be overlooked.

If you are in a leadership position at work, remember to model healthy break hygiene:

1. Incorporate breaks into the expected work schedule.

2. Model break-taking on a daily basis. Make sure you are seen with your yoga mat at lunchtime.

3. Provide on-site break activities that all can enjoy – an office dog for petting or walking, a calm lounge or a community puzzle table where all employees can stop to add a few pieces when rest is required.

Sometimes called 'the father of history', Greek historian Herodotus praised the Egyptian pharoah Amasis for understanding the importance of rest and pleasure. He described the pharoah as working in the morning and drinking, joking and being idle with his companions in the afternoon. When someone suggested he ought to behave in a more serious fashion, Amasis replied:

" *Men that have bows string them when they must use them, and unstring them when they have used them; were bows kept strung forever, they would break, and so could not be used when needed. Such, too, is the nature of man. Were one to be always at serious work and not permit oneself a bit of relaxation, he would go mad or idiotic before he knew it; I am well aware of that, and give each of the two its turn.* "

HERODOTUS
The Histories,

Restful habit: the pause

No matter how frantic your day, the restful pause can always be inserted into your schedule to create a moment of calm before the next event.

How to master 'the pause'

Simply close your eyes, slow your breathing, centre your body towards the earth and wait until your heart is beating at its faithful regular beat. Continue.

When to deploy 'the pause'

- At every threshold – before you leave the house and when you enter a new space.

- Before and after every journey, every meal and every difficult conversation.

" *Every now and then go away, have a little relaxation, for when you come back to your work your judgement will be surer. Go some distance away because then the work appears smaller and more of it can be taken in at a glance and a lack of harmony and proportion is more readily seen.* "

LEONARDO DA VINCI

"Adopt the pace of nature: her secret is patience."

RALPH WALDO EMERSON

Outdoor restful exercise

- Find a place of beauty to stop.

- Sit or lie, be still and listen.

- Feel the breeze, the sun on your skin.

- What does the world whisper back to you?

" Rest is not idleness, and to lie sometimes on the grass under trees on a summer's day, listening to the murmur of the water, or watching the clouds float across the sky, is by no means a waste of time."

JOHN LUBBOCK

The French playwright Molière suggested that all a person needs to be content is "a good bottle, a good book, a good friend." We can picture the scene quite clearly: a quiet room, a glass of wine, gentle reading and idle conversation with a companion.

Restful challenge

Create your own restful scene. Either describe the scene as if you were a novelist, send yourself a voice note or sketch out the restful situation as you imagine it.

Where would you be sitting/lying?

Who, if anyone, would be with you?

Would there be food or drink?

Would you be reading? Listening to music?

Place yourself at the peaceful heart of the scene – how does this make you feel?

Curl up and enjoy the literary convention in adventure novels whereby the main characters stop and rest in a safe space, gather their energy and continue on their journey to defeat their dastardly enemy. Just think of Mole and Ratty resting up in Badger's toasty home in *The Wind in the Willows*, or Harry Potter, Ron and Hermione stopping to revive themselves in Hagrid's hut, or tea with Lucy Pevensie and Mr Tumnus in *The Lion, The Witch and The Wardrobe*.

" The kindly Badger thrust them down on a settle to toast themselves at the fire, and bade them remove their wet coats and boots."

KENNETH GRAHAME
The Wind in the Willows

" *There is nothing more luxurious than eating while you read – unless it be reading while you eat.*"

E. NESBIT
The Magic World

Be like a character in a novel who needs a place to revive and replenish their energy, and create your own literary resting nook.

1. Establish your environment: favourite chair/beanbag/ window seat?

2. Accompany with delicious morsels to eat and drink.

3. Sit back, relax and enjoy.

There are people who keep cakes or an emergency pack of biscuits in the cupboard, or scones in the freezer, ready for an unexpected guest or impromptu tea party. These generous folk are ready to welcome friends and family and encourage them to sit down, take off their coats and relax into the warmth of a cheery rest and enjoy a plate of food. How easy is it to become such a person? What can we do to cultivate such warm hospitality?

" *There is an emanation from the heart in genuine hospitality which cannot be described, but is immediately felt and puts the stranger at once at his ease.*"

WASHINGTON IRVING

Am I a better lover when I am relaxed?

Am I a better parent when I am rested?

Am I a better friend when I am
at peace?

Am I a better colleague when I am
not stressed?

The answer is always **YES**: relaxation
is obligatory, not optional.

" Nothing is a greater impediment to being on good terms with others than being ill at ease with yourself."

HONORÉ DE BALZAC

Jot down how long it takes you to rest and reset. For some, a few star jumps and an espresso are sufficient to go again, for others, a more leisurely mocha and read of the news is what is required to restore equilibrium and tackle the next task. Find your restful sweet spot and diarize the time required.

Never rush an emotion...

Never hurry a feeling...

Never be hasty with your thoughts...

All of these platitudes reflect the deep wisdom that knows emotions and feelings require time to develop, settle and be understood. Avoid forcing feelings; give yourself permission to sit with emotions until the time comes to let them pass.

Be mindful of differing standards of rest for different people

While some are able to recharge with a cup of tea and a brisk walk, others require a long soak in the tub and an evening in front of the television. Avoid imposing your restful timings on others.

How to tell the difference between laziness and rest?

Rest is enjoyable while laziness weighs heavy with self-loathing. Once the initial luxury of indolence has worn off, few find much pleasure in prolonged periods of laziness.

At life's most poignant and challenging times we often find ourselves encouraged to 'move on' or 'return to normality', when perhaps what is required is a longer period of rest, recuperation or marinating in the new reality in which we have found ourselves. Consider those crucial times of childbirth, marriage and mourning for lost loved ones; how much better would we be able to cope with these changes if there was not a requirement to 'move on' or 'return to normality'.

Consider how our ancestors managed the challenging time of grieving. With no rush to 'move on', the Victorians had a useful mourning timetable that allocated suggested times required to 'get over' the loss of a loved one: a year for a parent and six months for a grandparent, for instance. Black would be worn for the first half, followed by 'half mourning' in mauve. Now of course such limits seem restrictive, but they demonstrate that we are unwise to rush grief – far better to encourage a more gentle and slower-paced return to equilibrium.

Restful exercise: understand the time required for big changes

Consider those transformative elements of your life where everything changes: leaving home, moving in, marriage, the birth of a baby, a new job, another baby, redundancy, loss of a parent, new job, a house move... and so on. Now, examine how much time should be spent on adjusting to such significant changes.

Be gentle with yourself and allow yourself time and rest to ease in to each new reality.

Don't be deceived: hurrying will never buy us more time.

When Pollyanna, the cheerful freckled orphan in the eponymous 1913 novel by Eleanor H. Porter, is sent to live with her Aunt Polly, she receives a lengthy list detailing how she will spend her day: reading, sewing, learning to cook and play music. Pollyanna cries out in dismay:

"Oh, but Aunt Polly, Aunt Polly, you haven't left me any time at all just to, to live."

"To live, child! What do you mean? As if you weren't living all the time!"

"Oh, of course I'd be breathing all the time I was doing those things, Aunt Polly, but I wouldn't be living... I mean living doing the things you want to do: playing outdoors, reading (to myself, of course), climbing hills... and finding out all about the houses and the people and everything everywhere... That's what I call living, Aunt Polly. Just breathing isn't living!"

Let us remember Pollyanna and her desire to just be; to walk, to talk to others, for she understands deeply that there is more to life than simply living, learning and working.

Saunter... stroll... amble... meander... wander... mosey... ramble... How many ways can you find of slowing down the pace of your daily walk?

Reframe resting from an *indulgence* to *training*

Just as you incorporate exercise and nutrition into your schedule, incorporate *rest* as a vital function of strength and conditioning training.

Understand the difference between winding down and rest. Give yourself sufficient time and space in which to wind down before you begin the important business of resting.

Admit it, most of us only have one way of relaxing, which is sitting somewhere soft watching a screen. Try to incorporate one other method of relaxation into your busy schedule and see which one is the most soothing.

Alternatives to screen-based relaxation

• Mindful colouring books

• Lying still listening to an audiobook

• Lego (yes, really)

• Knitting or crochet

• Jigsaw puzzling

• Model making

Restful idea: embrace the concept of deep play

We somehow think that playing ought to be only for children, but deep play – that blissful absorption in an activity – brings pleasure and benefits to adults too. The intense focus required alters our consciousness so that immediate worries are impossible to consider.

Ideas for deep restful play

- Playing musical instruments
- Singing
- Dancing
- Martial arts
- Chess
- Puzzles

Think outside traditionally gendered activities and unwind happily on the riverbank or inside a cluttered shed. Being beside water has long been known to offer a relaxing effect and engaging in close work can help the mind and body decompress.

Consider alternative methods to rest and rejuvenate

- Fly-fishing
- Woodwork
- Repairing household items
- Restoring a classic car or motorbike
- Chopping logs
- Yoga
- Flower arranging
- Baking a cake
- Jewellery making
- Embroidery

Restful challenge: when walking, look up not down

Just a small tilt of the head can be sufficient to adjust your mind from the fast business of walking forwards, to a more contemplative pace to arrive at your destination.

Sometimes our minds are not stilled by silent rest. Sometimes we need to distract and relax our over-thinking brains with strenuous activities. Rather than reaching for the bubble bath, pull on your boots and hike up the nearest hill, finally do that heavy lifting required in the garden or walk around the block as fast as you dare. Exerting the body can send waves of calm over the mind.

" Keep close to Nature's heart, yourself; and break clear away, once in awhile, and climb a mountain or spend a week in the woods. Wash your spirit clean."

JOHN MUIR

Rest idea: rest like an elite athlete

Embrace the protocols used by elite athletes whereby rest is prioritized just as much as training. After intense periods of training, elite athletes will generally rest for longer periods than mere mortals.

Reframe rest as elite-athlete training to help remove the guilt from enjoying a quiet, low-activity day.

Be inspired by elite athletes who embark on gentle wind-down activities, such as meditation, yoga, stretches and swimming on rest days to carefully promote blood flow and reduce muscle soreness.

Rest does not always need to be enjoyed in a horizontal position. Contemplate the concept of 'active rest'. What does this mean to you?

- Mindful cooking
- Steady-state cycling or rollerblading
- Yoga or pilates

Three ideas for active rest

- Walking in nature
- Tai chi and qigong
- Stretching exercises

Mantras to help encourage rest like an elite athlete

I am resting to optimize my mental and physical performance.

I am worthy of rest because my mind and body excel on a daily basis.

I am grateful for this rest day to recharge for ongoing excellence.

" In stillness the muddied water returns to clarity."

LAOZI

Be mindful of how your body moves from an active to a restful state. If your mind is agitated and leaping from one thought to another, refocus on bodily observations. Listen to your pulse rate, feel your eyes blinking. Once in tune with their rhythm, note how your pulse rate and blink rate lower as your body embraces a more restful state.

Quick fixes to relax exhausted bodies

1. Epsom salts in warm bathwater.

2. A hot water bottle across your shoulders.

3. Steam muscle stiffness away in the shower or steam room.

4. Self-massage by lying on the floor and rolling on a tennis ball.

5. Deep-tissue massage.

" Never be in a hurry; do everything quietly and in a calm spirit. Do not lose your inner peace for anything whatsoever, even if your whole world seems upset."

ST FRANCIS DE SALES

Restful charms and talismans

1. A silver cloud – to remind you that the storm will pass and rest will come.

2. A golden sun – to remind you that no matter how dark the storm, the sun will still rise tomorrow.

3. A silver moon – to remind you that sleep and rest are waiting to embrace you every night.

Nothing sours a moment of relaxation more than a disgruntled lover, child or friend asking when you'll be finished! Involve those closest to you in your bid to relax, explain to them your need for a break and ensure they are fully behind your chosen activity. Receiving their support and understanding for your absence has its own restful effect.

Restful idea: learn the fine art of pottering

Work and rest need not be so polarized. The fine art of pottering – *to move or go about in a casual way* – is a lovely halfway house between the two that should be embraced. Pottering is restful work or working rest, that wonderful experience of idly doing this or that with no fixed goal. From these magical moments, minds and bodies can relax and rejuvenate.

Six places to potter

1. A greenhouse
2. An allotment
3. A crafting studio
4. The patio
5. The garden
6. The local market town

(Never the kitchen or office or any other space where real work beckons.)

" It is awfully hard work doing nothing. "

OSCAR WILDE

Restful inspiration: revive the Victorian craze for carving 'Rest and Be Thankful' on to benches, settles or fireside chairs. Next time you are upcycling a vintage piece of furniture, consider stencilling this restful aphorism on to your repainted piece. And after all the hard work, sit back, rest and be thankful.

Within our minds there lurks a little imp who whispers as we are about to relax: "*You should be doing…*" Learn to discipline this imp and put all your 'shoulds' on hold.

Rest understands that...

Not every meal needs
to be photographed

Not every scene needs to
be curated

Not every moment needs to
be captured

Rest understands the importance of...

Privacy

Silence

Logging off

" Simplify your life. Don't waste the years struggling for things that are unimportant. Don't burden yourself with possessions. Keep your needs and wants simple and enjoy what you have. Don't destroy your peace of mind by looking back, worrying about the past. Live in the present. Simplify! "

HENRY DAVID THOREAU

Escape the default setting to organize

An empty afternoon?

A cancelled evening event?

A free weekend?

Resist the urge to organize alternative activities. Don't call anyone. Don't arrange anything. Just rest and enjoy the unexpected space.

Doing nothing is not always nothing.
Doing nothing is space where
inspiration is born.

" What I like doing best is Nothing."

" How do you do Nothing,"
asked Pooh after he had wondered
for a long time.

" Well, it's when people call out at
you just as you're going off to do it,
'What are you going to do, Christopher
Robin?' and you say, 'Oh, Nothing,' and
then you go and do it. It means just
going along, listening to all the things
you can't hear, and not bothering."

A.A. MILNE

Be inspired by Christopher Robin's joy in doing nothing

What is your idea of doing nothing?

Where would you be?

Who would accompany you?

What would you see?

How would you feel?

" Doing nothing is sometimes one of the highest of the duties of man."

G.K. CHESTERTON

Dolce far niente

Relax like the Italians and enjoy the 'sweetness of doing nothing'.

無心 (Mushin)

Discover the Japanese concept of 無心 (mushin) that roughly translates as 'no mind' or a mind free from anger, thoughts and ego. Rooted in Zen Buddhism and Japanese martial arts, mushin is the ultimate concept of inner peace, where there is neither past nor future, only the empty present.

Studies on those who experience mushin show transient hypofrontality – a temporary decrease in pre-frontal cortex activity – that part of our brain that deals with rational thought.

無爲 (Wu wei)

The ancient Chinese concept of wu wei is the art of non-doing or doing nothing. This is not an invitation to relax forever but rather not to force your ego on the way of the universe. A central principle of Taoism, wu wei asks that we respect the flow of the universe and allow ourselves and events to unfold naturally so that our actions are aligned with the natural rhythm of the way (Tao). Fostering such harmony will lead to greater chances of fulfilment.

" *Life is a series of natural and spontaneous changes. Don't resist them; that only creates sorrow. Let reality be reality. Let things flow naturally forward in whatever way they like.*"

LAOZI

Siesta – that indulgent snooze after a long lunch in the Mediterranean sun – is a Spanish word derived from *hora sexta* – Latin for 'sixth hour.' The Romans divided the day into 12 hours, counting from dawn, with the *hora sexta* falling around midday – the perfect time for a light lunch and hour of rest.

Can't we just picture the scene of a Spanish town at slumber: men nodding off in doorways, boys snoozing under a tree, the town dogs stretched out in the shade, and behind billowing lace curtains the women dozing inside. Let us embrace the Mediterranean languor of the Spanish siesta and not reduce it to a cold and clinical 'power nap'.

" *In summer, after his midday meal, he took some fruit and a single draught and then, taking off his clothes and boots, just as he was accustomed to do at night, he would rest for two or three hours.* "

EINHARD
10th-century description of Emperor
Charlemagne's routine

Winston Churchill was a devoted fan of the siesta, requiring a two-hour nap after lunch throughout the Second World War. He cited this practice as one of the habits that enabled him to cope with the mighty pressure of defeating fascism.

Not to be confused with the Spanish siesta, the Italian pennica is a short, post-lunch nap, taken while still dressed. Enjoyed by older generations in central and southern regions, the pennica lasts for a brief 20 minutes and is sufficient to shake off the torpor that follows a delicious lunch.

Consider the Scandinavian approach and take your afternoon nap outside in startlingly cold conditions. Choose a spot out of direct wind, wrap up warmly and let the weak rays of the sun shower you with vitamin D.

Q: Fancy improving your mood and your physical and cognitive performances, along with feeling less stressed and more alert?

A: Take an afternoon nap

(Yes really – it's that simple! Multiple scientific studies show the deep benefits of short 20–30-minute naps. Go on, try one now.)

Be like the English and savour the deep rest that a nice cup of tea brings. Momentary peace and reassurance in your favourite cup. Heaven.

"I am so fond of tea that I could write a whole dissertation on its virtues. It comforts and enlivens without the risks attendant on spirituous liquors. Gentle herb! Let the florid grape yield to thee. Thy soft influence is a more safe inspirer of social joy."

JAMES BOSWELL

Six restful items in which to make a relaxing investment

1. A hammock

2. A table next to the hammock at exactly the right height for hot or cold drinks and a small bowl of nibbles

3. A yoga mat

4. A weighted blanket

5. An essential oil diffuser

6. A rocking chair

Create sumptuous sleep stations by extending the places in the house where naps may be enjoyed. Be it a window seat, bean bag or outdoor garden egg chair, ensure that all possible sleep stations are comfortably furnished with necessary cushions and blankets. Never underestimate the power of well-placed soft furnishings to sooth the soul.

" There is nothing like staying at home for real comfort."

JANE AUSTEN

Find rest in the natural pauses of the day

Without our arranging it, there are natural pauses in the day that we have fallen into the habit of rushing through in our quest for ever-greater achievements and pleasures. Mealtimes are the most obvious markers that call for a pause in life's hectic rush. Think carefully about what other natural pauses can be found in the day, and what can be done to embellish these once peaceful times.

Breakfast at leisure.

Lunch outside in the sunshine.

Enjoy dinner with friends and family.

Stretch yourself awake with
morning yoga or a solitary walk.

Nap for 20 minutes after lunch.

Read quietly before bed.

*" Think in the morning. Act in the noon.
Eat in the evening. Sleep in the night."*

WILLIAM BLAKE

Create a bowl of restful ideas

Fill a bowl with creative ideas for rest, such as forest bathing, hand massages or homemade face masks. Take it in turns with your family or friends to pull out a restful idea at the start of each week and help each other to make time and enjoy. Don't forget your turn!

Host a restival

Arrange a grown-up sleepover focused entirely on rest. Order take-out so no-one has to cook and invite your closest friends for a rest-based indulgence session. Facemasks, pedicures, hand massages, the whole restful caboodle in one room so no-one has to move terribly far.

Keeping hands busy is a quick hack to keep minds quiet. Don't be afraid of returning to childhood activities that offer a creative outlet for your hands and a period of rest for your mind.

Origami

Painting by numbers

Polymer clay modelling

Embroidering and upcycling clothes

Scrapbooking

"And he that can take rest is greater than he who can take cities."

BENJAMIN FRANKLIN

Don't be afraid of prioritizing rest. All three of the major Abrahamic religions feature God resting on the seventh day 'from all his work that he had made'.

The seventh day of rest is sanctified and we are encouraged to follow the creator's example and *rest*, for one day, each and every week. Imagine how much more rested both physically, mentally and spiritually society would be if we managed to follow this ancient instruction.

Remember the ancient holy command to rest one day out of seven

Six days shalt thou labour, and do all thy work: But the seventh day is the sabbath of the Lord thy God: in it thou shalt not do any work, thou, nor thy son, nor thy daughter, thy manservant, nor thy maidservant, nor thy cattle, nor thy stranger that is within thy gates: For in six days the Lord made heaven and earth, the sea, and all that in them is, and rested the seventh day: wherefore the Lord blessed the sabbath day, and hallowed it.

KING JAMES BIBLE
Genesis

Restful idea: reclaim the day of rest

- Keep one day of the weekend entirely empty.

- No large lunch parties.

- No sports commitments.

- Just you, your loved ones and time together.

How to intentionally plan a day of rest

- Turn off all phones and devices.

- Pre-prepare food, so only reheating is required.

- Go old school and dig out board games and jigsaws.

- Get comfy with fiction, magazines or sketch books.

- Slow down, and avoid rushing the day.

- Expect nothing or yourself or others.

Sitting, reclining and resting are the most common positions for the Buddha to be depicted. Eyes closed, in a state of nirvana, Buddha statues embody the importance of rest for achieving enlightenment.

" Wishing: In gladness and in safety,

May all beings be at ease.

Whatever living being there may be;

Whether weak or strong,

Out of sight or near,

Or hidden or revealed,

May all beings be at ease."

THE BUDDHA
Karaniya Metta Sutta: The Discourse
on Loving Kindness

Try chanting the Tibetan mantra to induce sleep, some say as many as 108 times:

" Ri Ah Hung "

Place a resting Buddha at your work station as a gentle prompt to help you elevate rest and meditation in order to achieve those blissful states of peace and tranquillity.

" The calm man is not the man who is dull. The calm man is the one who has control over the mind waves. Activity is the manifestation of inferior strength, calmness, of the superior."

SWAMI VIVEKANANDA

"A truly Krishna conscious person, always absorbed in Transcendence, in constant undisturbed meditation on his worship-able Lord, is as steady as a lamp in a windless place. Just as the flame is not agitated, the mind is not agitated, and that steadiness is the perfection of yoga."

BHAGAVAD GITA

How easy is it to be as peaceful as a lamp in a windless place?

Guru Argan Dev, the fifth Guru of the Sikh religion, composed the Sukhmani Sahib, a poetic and spiritual guide on how to find peace in a turbulent world. The word Sukhmani means 'consoler of the mind'. Listen to recitations of the Sukhmani Sahib to help guide your mind towards a restful state.

" *Meditate, meditate, meditate in remembrance of Him, and find peace. Worry and anguish, shall be dispelled from your body.*"

FROM THE SUKHMANI SAHIB

" *It is said that the effect of eating too much lettuce is 'soporific'.*

I have never felt sleepy after eating lettuces; but then I am not a rabbit.

They certainly had a very soporific effect upon the Flopsy Bunnies! "

BEATRIX POTTER
The Tale of the Flopsy Bunnies

In her charming tale of the Flopsy Bunnies, who fall asleep after eating too much lettuce, Beatrix Potter claims that lettuce is 'soporific' (tending to induce drowsiness or sleep) and science has proved her to be correct. When you next snap the stem of a lettuce, make note of the milky juice that seeps out – this is lactucarium, a substance that has mild sedative qualities.

Embrace space-age and ancient technology to improve your night's sleep. Adorn your bedside table with one of these plants listed by NASA to help purify air:

- **Snake plant** (Sansevieria trifasciata)
- **Peace lily** (Spathiphyllum)
- **English ivy** (Hedera helix)
- **Aloe vera** (Aloe barbadensis miller)
- **Boston fern** (Nephrolepis exaltata)
- **Spider plant** (Chlorophytum comosum)
- **Bamboo palm** (Chamaedorea seifrizii)
- **Dracaena** (Dracaena spp.)
- **Areca palm** (Dypsis lutescens)
- **Gerbera daisy** (Gerbera jamesonii)
- **Chinese evergreen** (Aglaonema)

Lavender oil is known for its restful qualities, but did you know these other plants share similar properties? When next refreshing your oil burner or bath oil supplies, consider:

Jasmine. With its gloriously uplifting fragrance, jasmine can help lift moods and encourage feelings of peace.

Sandalwood. As a relaxant, sandalwood can calm the nervous system and thus encourage sleep.

Melissa. Also known as lemon balm, this eases pain and indigestion, and is said to support stress reduction and promote sleep.

Three ways to build restful lavender into your bedtime routine

1. Keep your sleepwear folded with a lavender bag for an all-encompassing aroma.

2. Rub one of two drops of lavender oil in the palms of your hands. Inhale and announce your night-time mantras.

3. Apply tiny drops of lavender oil to your temples as an anointing ritual at bedtime.

Mentally fatigued? Try burning clary sage. Well known for its ability to calm the mind with its deep, musky aroma, clary sage can be burned or diffused while bathing before bed.

And if you are the sort to be sceptical of herbal claims, understand that our olfactory nerves are powerful. Repeatedly associating one particular aroma with sleep can prompt the mind and body to relax out of habit.

Being mindful to avoid caffeine or alcohol too close to bedtime, warming drinks have long been known to soothe the senses before bed. Incorporate them into your sleep hygiene system as a cue to your body that it's time to wind down.

Warm cocoa (using cocoa powder rather than drinking chocolate which has a high sugar content).

Warm milk and honey.

Chamomile, valerian or peppermint teas.

Why should bedtime stories be just for children?

If you share your bed with someone, could you also share your book? Consider reading the same book aloud to each other. It's a deeply intimate activity that encourages relaxation and a separation of the concerns of the day from the peace of the night.

Be aware that keeping very active crystals such as cinnabar or malachite near your bed can interrupt rest, as their powerful vibrations interfere with your lowered energy levels. Instead, choose soothing crystals to keep at your bedside or under your pillow.

- Amethyst
- Celestite
- Agate
- Moonstone
- Obsidian

Consider meditating with the crystals before entering the realm of sleep.

"A ruffled mind makes a restless pillow."

CHARLOTTE BRONTË

" *Now, blessings light on him that first invented sleep! It covers a man all over, thoughts and all, like a cloak; it is meat for the hungry, drink for the thirsty, heat for the cold, and cold for the hot. It is the current coin that purchases all the pleasures of the world cheap, and the balance that sets the king and the shepherd, the fool and the wise man, even.* "

MIGUEL DE CERVANTES

The first step to healthy sleep is to purposely invite healthy sleep into your routine. Try this mantra:

As I embark on a journey towards night-time rest, I invite relaxation and sleep into my bed, my body and my mind.

Sleeping is *not* cheating!

Five reasons why adults need seven to nine hours' sleep a night:

1. **Sleep embeds and consolidates memories**: during sleep, our brains process information from the day and transfer it to our long-term memory bank.

2. **Sleep repairs the body**: while sleeping, our bodies busily repair tissues and cells.

3. **Sleep boosts the immune system**: sustained good sleeping sessions help the body fight off infection.

4. **Sleep regulates hormones**: prolonged and sustained sleep helps to balance the hormones that control appetite, mood and those vital energy levels (don't we just know it!).

5. **Sleep improves mood**: sleep deprivation can lead to irritability, anxiety and depression – we've all been there in a morning fury after a sleepless night!

Try not to worry if you're struggling to sleep – the very act of lying in bed is still beneficial for rest. That soothing thought is often sufficient to encourage sleep's tender embrace.

Meet Morpheus, an ancient Greek god of dreams and sleep. He was the son of Hypnos (sleep) and Nyx (night). If sleep still eludes you – send up a prayer to ancient Morpheus.

*" Enjoy the honey-heavy
dew of slumber.*

Thou hast no figures, nor no fantasies,

*Which busy care draws in the brains of
men;*

Therefore thou sleep'st so sound."

WILLIAM SHAKESPEARE
Julius Caesar

Here Shakespeare is observing that the sweetest sleep is had by those who have no worries or cares to torment their dreams.

Don't forget that we spend one third of our lives – on average 26 years – asleep.

"I divide my time as follows: half the time I sleep, the other half I dream. I never dream when I sleep, for that would be a pity, for sleeping is the highest accomplishment of genius."

SØREN KIERKEGAARD

*" There is a time for many words
and there is also a time for sleep."*

HOMER

Three restful mantras to say at bedtime

I give permission for this rest time to embrace me and walk me gently to the land of sleep.

With gratitude in my heart, I enter my warm and inviting bed to rest.

I leave the worries of the day at the door and rest for tomorrow.

" *When a man looks long at [the stars]... he grows calm and forgets small things. They answer his questions and show him that his earth is only one of the million worlds. Hold your soul still and look upward often, and you will understand their speech. Never forget the stars.*"

FRANCES HODGSON BURNETT
The Land of The Blue Flower

" Sleep! O gentle sleep!
Nature's soft nurse."

WILLIAM SHAKESPEARE
Henry VI, Part II

" Finish each day and be done with it. You have done what you could. Some blunders and absurdities no doubt crept in; forget them as soon as you can. Tomorrow is a new day; begin it well and serenely and with too high a spirit to be encumbered with your old nonsense."

RALPH WALDO EMERSON

" My troubles are all over and I am at home."

ANNA SEWELL
Black Beauty

QUOTES ARE TAKEN FROM

A.A. Milne, 1882–1956,
English author and playwright

Abraham Lincoln, 1809–1865,
16th president of the United States

Anna Sewell, 1820–1878, English novelist

Beatrix Potter, 1866–1943,
English author and illustrator

Benjamin Franklin, 1706–1790,
American polymath

Buddha, 6th–4th century BCE,
Indian philosopher and founder of Buddhism

Charles Dickens, 1812–1870, English novelist

Charlotte Brontë, 1816–1855, English novelist

E. Nesbit, 1858–1924, English author

Einhard, c. 770–c. 840, Frankish historian

Etty Hillesum, 1914–1943, Dutch writer and diarist

Frances Hodgson Burnett, 1849–1924,
English–American writer

G. K. Chesterton, 1874–1936,
English writer and philosopher

Henry David Thoreau, 1817–1862,
American essayist, poet and philosopher

Herodotus, c. 484–c. 425 BCE, Greek historian

Homer, c. 8th century BCE,
ancient Greek epic poet

Honoré de Balzac, 1799–1850, French novelist

Ivan Turgenev, 1818–1883, Russian novelist

James Boswell, 1740–1795, Scottish writer

Jane Austen, 1775–1817, English novelist

John Lubbock, 1st Baron Avebury, 1834–1913,
English banker, politician, scientist and
archaeologist

John Muir, 1838–1914, Scottish–American naturalist and author

Julie Jeanne Éléonore de Lespinasse, 1732–1776, French salon hostess

Kenneth Grahame, 1859–1932, British writer

Laozi, 6th century BCE, Chinese philosopher

Leo Tolstoy, 1828–1910, Russian writer

Leonardo da Vinci, 1452–1519, Italian polymath

Lucy Maud Montgomery, 1874–1942, Canadian author

Mahatma Gandhi, 1869–1948, Indian lawyer, anti-colonial nationalist and civil-rights activist

Margaret Fuller, 1810–1850, American writer, critic and feminist

Miguel de Cervantes, 1547–1616, Spanish writer

Nikolai Gogol, 1809–1852, Russian writer

Oscar Wilde, 1854–1900, Irish poet and playwright

Ovid, 43 BCE–17 CE, Roman poet

Ralph Waldo Emerson, 1803–1882,
American essayist

Søren Kierkegaard, 1813–1855, Danish philosopher

St Francis de Sales, 1567–1622,
French bishop and writer

Swami Vivekananda, 1863–1902,
Indian Hindu monk and philosopher

Washington Irving, 1783–1859, American writer
and diplomat

William Blake, 1757–1827,
English poet, artist, and printmaker

William Shakespeare, 1564–1616,
English playwright, poet and actor

USEFUL BOOKS

Burnout: How to Manage Your Nervous System Before it Manages You, Dr Claire Plumbly, Yellow Kite. 2024

The Rest Revolution: How to Reclaim Your Rhythm and Conquer Burnout When Overworking Has Become the Norm, Amanda Miller Littlejohn, Wiley, 2024

Why We Sleep: The New Science of Sleep and Dreams, Matthew Walker, Penguin, 2017

USEFUL WEBSITES

www.lifehack.org

www.mind.org.uk

www.nhs.uk

www.headspace.com

Managing Director Sarah Lavelle
Assistant Editors Sofie Shearman and
Ellie Spence
Words Joanna Gray
Series Designer Emily Lapworth
Designer Katy Everett
Head of Production Stephen Lang
Production Controller Martina Georgieva

Quadrille, Penguin Random House UK, One Embassy Gardens, 8 Viaduct Gardens, London SW11 7BW

Quadrille Publishing Limited is part of the Penguin Random House group of companies whose addresses can be found at global. penguinrandomhouse.com

Penguin
Random House
UK

Published by Quadrille in 2025

www.penguin.co.uk

A CIP catalogue record for this book is available from the British Library

ISBN 978 1 83783 289 7

10 9 8 7 6 5 4 3 2 1

Printed in China by RR Donnelley Asia Printing Solution Limited

The authorised representative in the EEA is Penguin Random House Ireland, Morrison Chambers, 32 Nassau Street, Dublin D02 YH68.